Heinemann EXPLORE Science

Student Book

New International Edition

Grade 1

Tara Lievesley, Deborah Herridge
Series editor: John Stringer

ALWAYS LEARNING

PEARSON

Pearson Education Limited is a company incorporated in England and Wales having its registered office at Edinburgh Gate, Harlow, Essex, CM20 2JE.

Registered company number: 872828

www.pearsonglobalschools.com

Text © Pearson Education Limited 2012
First published 2003. This edition published 2012

16 15 14 13 12
IMP 10 9 8 7 6 5 4 3 2 1

British Library Cataloguing in Publication Data
A catalogue record for this book is available from the British Library

ISBN 978 0 435133 55 9

Edited by Anna Woodford and Janice Curry
Designed and typeset by Scout Design Associates
Original illustrations © Pearson Education Limited, 2003, 2009, 2012
Illustrated by Kevin Hopgood, Beehive Illustration Ltd
Cover photo © Alamay Images
Indexed by Indexing Specialists (UK) Ltd
Printed in Malaysia, CTP-KHL

Acknowledgements

The author and publisher would like to thank the following individuals and organisations for permission to reproduce photographs:

(Key: b-bottom; c-centre; l-left; r-right; t-top)

Alamy Images: 9tl, 15tr, 16tr, 19tr, 28br, 33c, 41l, 42 (swimming), 44c, 44br, 45tl; Arabian Eye: 42 (cricket), 42 (football), 42 (Skateboard); Fotolia.com: 4 (Cheese), 4 (Kababs), 5c, 8 (goat), 8 (woman), 8br, 14bl, 15 (Carrots), 15br, 18c, 19c, 19bl, 21 (bricks), 21 (bucket), 21 (Cutlery), 21 (Jar), 21 (Scarf), 21bl, 22 (kettle), 22 (pouch), 22tr, 23tc, 23tr, 23bl, 25tr, 26cr, 28 (boots), 28 (coat), 28 (flip flops), 28 (gloves), 28 (t shirt), 29cl, 33tl, 34bl, 46bl, 49 (Flute), 49 (Violin), 54r, 55cr, 56br; Getty Images: 8 (dolphins), 37br, 50cl; Glow Images: 1cr, 2cl, 2bl, 8 (Dolphin), 8 (Horse head), 10tc, 13bc, 20t, 20b, 35br, 39bl, 40cr, 41c, 41r, 41bl, 42tr; Pearson Education Ltd: Trevor Clifford 14tr, Photolink. Photodisc 14l, 49 (drums); Science Photo Library Ltd: 20r, 26bl; Shutterstock.com: 2 (rock), 4 (eggs), 4 (pineapple), 4 (Rice), 4cl, 6bl, 7bl, 7bc, 8 (baby), 8 (horse), 9 (Frog), 9tc, 9tr, 9c (tadpole), 9bl, 10c, 10cl, 10cr, 10br, 11br, 12bl, 12br, 13tr, 13l, 13br, 14c, 14cl, 14bc, 18bl, 22bl, 23tl, 23bc, 23br, 26tl, 26tr, 26c, 27cl, 29tl, 29bl, 29bc, 32t, 32l, 32r, 32b, 33b, 33br, 38bl, 43br, 44tr, 44l, 48l, 48br, 53cr

All other images © Pearson Education

Every effort has been made to contact copyright holders of material reproduced in this book. Any omissions will be rectified in subsequent printings if notice is given to the publishers. In some instances we have been unable to trace the owners of copyright material, and we would appreciate any information that would enable us to do so.

Contents

How to use this book

At the beginning of each Unit there are lists of things you should already know or be able to do.

Think about this question. By the end of the Unit you will know how to answer it.

This shows words that are important. Learn and use them.

Unit 2: Growing plants

What do you know?
- Humans and other animals grow.
- They change as they grow.

Skills check

Can you...
- point to a plant?
- name a **flower**?
- name some vegetables you eat?

Let's find out...

Why do we call some plants **weeds**?

Words to learn

alive	petals
bark	root
chart	seed
dead	stem
flower	tree
fruit	veins
grow	wilt
leaf	water
light	

This box tells you what the lesson is about.

Find out what coloured words mean in the Glossary at the back of the book.

Dead or alive?

Things to learn
- If a plant is alive.
- If plastic plants can grow.
- To compare living and non-living things.

I wonder...

Will a plastic **flower** grow if you plant it?

Are plants alive?

No, they don't eat.

But they grow. They need water too.

Dig deeper

Find out:
- how you can make seeds grow faster?

Things to do

Wet some cotton wool. Drop a few **seeds** onto it. Put it on the window sill. What happens? Are seeds alive?

Did you know?
- Seeds change with warmth and water!

Plenty of plants

Things to learn
- Where plants grow.
- The names of some plants.
- To explore and observe your world.

I live here

Plants live in many places. Different plants live in different places.

They live where they grow best.

I wonder...

Is there anywhere that plants don't grow?

Things to do

What plants live where? Explore a garden or park. How many plants can you name?

Dig deeper

Find out:
- if all plants have **flowers**.

Did you know?
- Some plants eat animals!

Sunflowers grow in warm sunny places

Me too!

Animals live in many places too. They need plants for food and for homes.

Some monkeys live high in trees and eat the trees' fruit

Try these activities. Your teacher will help.

These boxes give you some fascinating facts.

This box tells you what you will find out. Your teacher will help you.

Use what you have learned to answer these questions.

Check what you have learned.

Here you find answers to important questions.

What did you find?

Sheila and Habiba drew these pictures.

	Day 1	Day 2	Day 3	Day 4	Day 5
Plants under cloth					
Plants in sunlight					

Which plants grew better? How can you tell?

Which plant was grown in the warmer place?

Did you know?
- Plants grow best in a warm place.

Seeds inside

Things to learn
- Where plants grow from.
- To explore how plants grow.
- To record your work.

I wonder…
What makes a seed start to grow?

Is my plant alive?
We know plants are alive. Sometimes plants look dead but they contain seeds, which can grow into new plants.

Soy bean plant seed pods

Poppy seed pods

Which comes first?
When a seed is planted and watered, it grows. It sends out a root and then a shoot.

Things to do
Plant a seed. Watch how it grows. Draw pictures of it. Mix them up. Ask your friend to put them back in order.

Dig deeper
Find out:
- Where the seeds are on a strawberry?

Did you know?
- Seeds can start to grow in the dark.

Unit 2: Review

What have you learned?
- Where we find plants.
- The names of the parts of a plant.
- What some of the parts are for.
- How plants grow.
- How a seed starts to grow.

Find out more about…
- other animals' life cycles
- whether a plant is alive or not.

Check-up
How can you tell if a plant or animal is alive?

Even the weeds in the garden are living plants.

The answer!
A weed is a plant. Weeds grow where we don't want them!

Unit 1: Ourselves and other animals

How are you like your friends? More than you think! We all have the same arms and legs, ears, noses and mouths. How can you tell who is who?

What do you know?

- We are all alike.
- We all have arms and legs.
- Some of us have brothers and sisters.

Words to learn

adult	grow	sight
alike	hear	similar
animal	human	smell
arm	leg	tall/taller/tallest
beak	living	taste
chart	myself	tongue
different	nose	touch
ear	old/older	wing
eye	sense	young/younger
feel	see	

Let's find out...

Can you tell who someone is without looking?

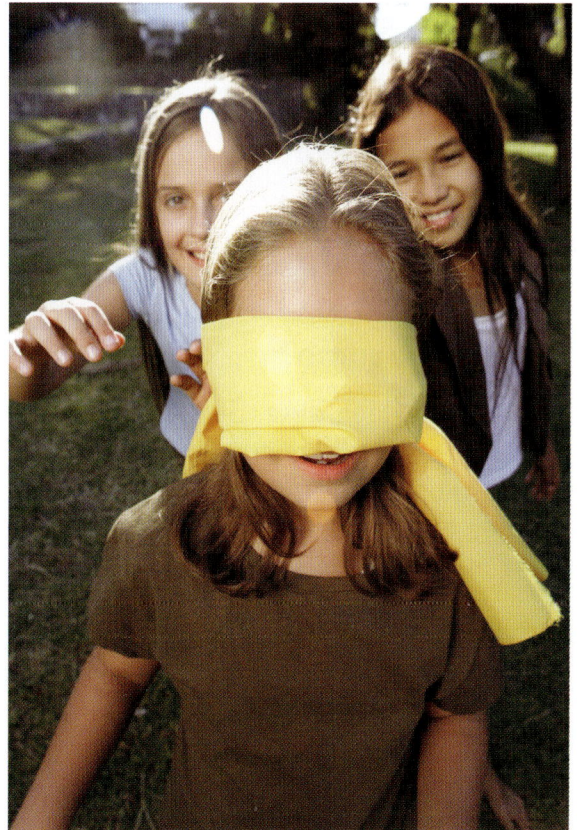
Who is behind you?

I'm special!

Things to learn

- If something is alive or not.
- How we are the same and different.
- To compare things.

Alive or not

You are **alive**. You move, eat and grow.
A horse is alive. A rock isn't alive.

Which is alive?

Are we the same?

All **humans** look alike. But all humans
are **different**. All children have hair. But
not all the same colour.

How are we the same?

Things to do

Draw your face. Colour your eyes and
hair. Does your friend have the same
colour eyes or hair? The same shaped
nose? Label the face parts.

Dig deeper

Find out:
- how many different eye colours
  there are in your class.

I wonder...

Can you tell which
twin is which?

What differences
can you see?

Did you know?

- All hair is a shade of brown.

Who's tallest?

Your challenge

- To compare the heights of different children.
- To think about what will happen.
- To record your work.

I'm older so I'm taller.

But my younger sister is taller than me!

If you are older you should be taller.

What to do

The children in class 1 want to find out if the oldest person is always the tallest. They line up in order of age.

What you need

- a blank wall to lean against
- paper to put against the wall
- a pencil

What to check

Now try it yourselves.

- Line up your class in order of age.
- Mark their height on the paper.

When is your birthday?

You are taller, move up there.

How old are you?

Who is right? How can we find out?

What did you find?

- Is the oldest child in your class the tallest?
- Is the youngest child the smallest?

Did you know?

- Your hair and nails grow all your life.

Healthy food

Things to learn

- What foods are healthy.
- What drinks are healthy.
- To share what you find.

I wonder…

How long we can live without food or water?

Good food

This meal has foods that keep us healthy.

Which foods can you name?

Eating Breakfast

Your biggest meal each day should be breakfast.

What do you eat for breakfast?

Things to do

Food can be grouped. Sort out these foods into groups. What would you call these groups?

There are different food groups. Take something from each group. Make it into a meal.

Did you know?

- You need a 'balanced' diet – something from each food group – to be healthy.

Staying healthy

Things to learn
- What some foods help you do.
- Why you should eat less of some types of food.

Different foods

Some foods give you energy. Some foods help you grow. Some foods keep you healthy. Some foods add fat.

How do you grow?

Eat good like meat and fish to grow. Eat fruit and vegetables to be healthy.

You don't just grow on your birthday

With the right diet you grow tall but not fat.

Things to do
- What foods do you eat most? Ask your class for their favourite food. Make a chart of what they say.

Dig deeper
Find out:
- what happens if you eat too much fat

I wonder…

Will I keep growing if I eat lots of foods that make me grow?

Did you know?
- Raw fruit and vegetables are healthier than cooked ones.

Give me five senses

Things to learn

- What our senses are called.
- Where our senses are.
- To observe senses.

I wonder…

Why do some people wear glasses?

The five senses

You have five **senses**. They are **touch**, **smell**, **taste**, **sight** and **hearing**. They help us to know about the world around us.

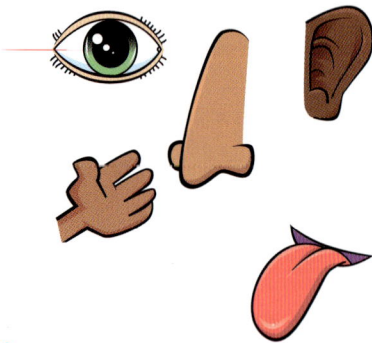

I spy…

Two eyes help us to pick things up. Close one eye. Pick up a pin from the floor. It is more difficult with one eye.

Light enters our eye

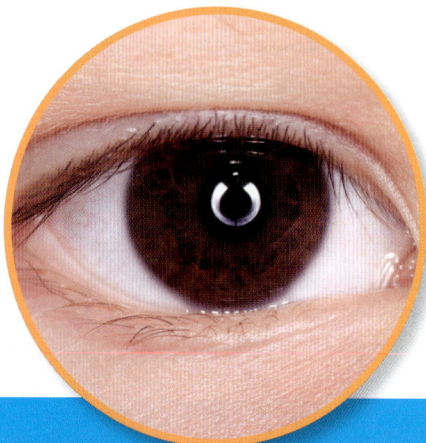

Things to do

How well can you see? What is the smallest letter you can read?

E, F, P…

E
FP
TOZ
HPEX

Dig deeper

Find out:
- how **blind** people 'read'.

Did you know?

- Loud noises can damage your ears.

I'm sensitive

Things to learn

- How our senses help us.
- How we are like other animals.
- To explore senses.

I wonder…

What if I couldn't feel anything?

What's that smell?

Our eyes see. Our ears hear. What does our nose do?

Our nose smells good and bad things

Things to do

Can you name a food without seeing it? How can you tell what it is? What if you hold your nose?

Does the colour of food affect taste or smell? How can you test it?

Hissss

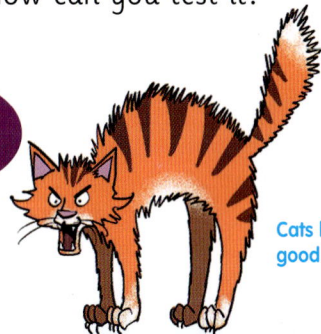

Cats have very good hearing

Extra sense

All animals have the same senses. Goats and tigers hear, taste, smell, see and feel.

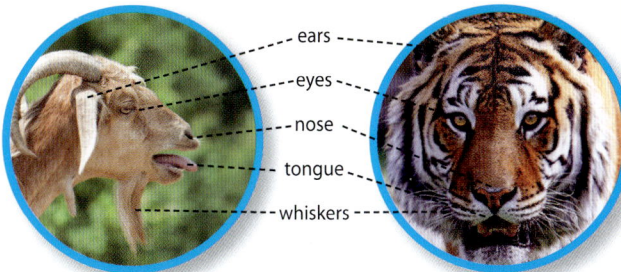

ears
eyes
nose
tongue
whiskers

All animals have senses too

Dig deeper

Find out:
- about any other senses

Did you know?

- Some animals can hear and see better than us.

Growing older

Things to learn

- How we grow.
- To compare us with other animals.
- How we change as we get older.

I wonder...

Do all parts of your body grow?

What would happen if we didn't stop growing?

That's not my mummy

We look like our family. Other animals look like their families.

Who's my mummy?

Things to do

Look at pictures of you as a baby. How have you changed as you got older?

Dig deeper

Find out:
- if all animals change as they get older.

Getting older

As we get older we change. We grow taller. What else changes?

Did you know?

- Some animals lay eggs. When they hatch, baby ducks follow their mother.

We all grow

We are animals

Like all animals, humans grow and change. They may have babies. They die. This is called their **life cycle**.

Whose baby?

Some animals lay eggs. The babies may be very different from their parents

These animals change as they grow older

What have you learned?

- The names of parts of your body.
- What your five senses are.
- How you change as you grow.
- What we need to grow healthy.

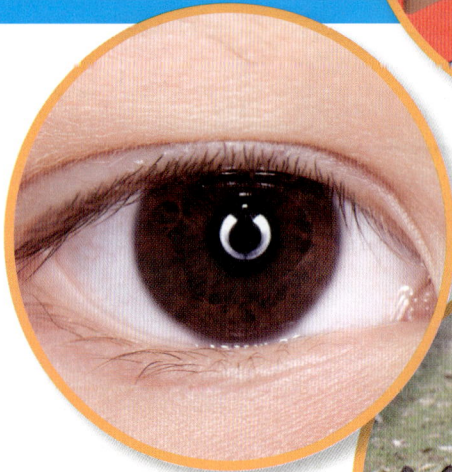

Find out more about...

- other animals' life cycles
- if plants are alive or not.

Check-up

How do you know that humans are animals?

The answer!

How can you tell who is next to you with your eyes shut?

You can use your other senses, even your ears!

What do you know?

- Humans and other animals grow.
- They change as they grow.

Let's find out...

Why do we call some plants **weeds**?

Words to learn

alive	petals
bark	root
chart	seed
dead	stem
flower	tree
fruit	veins
grow	wilt
leaf	water
light	

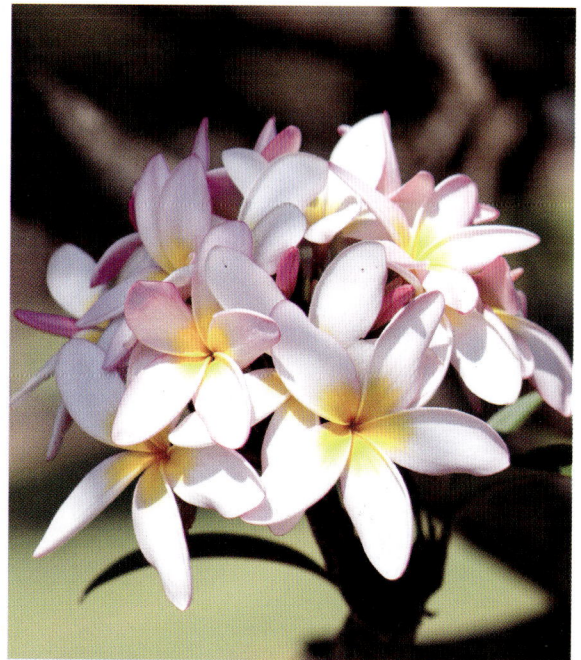

Dead or alive?

Things to learn

- If a plant is alive.
- If plastic plants can grow.
- To compare living and non-living things.

I wonder...

Will a plastic flower grow if you plant it?

Are plants alive?

No, they don't eat.

But they grow. They need water too.

Dig deeper

Find out:
- how you can make seeds grow faster.

Things to do

Wet some cotton wool. Drop a few **seeds** onto it. Put it on the window sill.

What happens? Are seeds **alive**?

These are carob seeds

Did you know?

- Seeds change with warmth and water!

Plenty of plants

Things to learn
- Where plants grow.
- The names of some plants.
- To explore and observe your world.

I wonder...

Is there anywhere that plants don't grow?

I live here

Plants live in many places. Different plants live in different places.

They live where they grow best.

Sunflowers grow in warm sunny places

Things to do

What plants live where? Explore a garden or park. How many plants can you name?

Dig deeper

Find out:
- if all plants have flowers.

Did you know?

- Some plants eat animals!

Me too!

Animals live in many places too. They need plants for food and for homes.

Some monkeys live high in trees and eat the trees' fruit

Plant parts

Things to learn

- The names of parts of a plant.
- Compare different plants.
- Decide what to do.

I wonder…

Are all stems and leaves green?

flower

bud

leaf

stem

roots

The parts of a plant

What am I?

Look at different plants. Use these words to label their parts:

stem   leaf   flower   root   bud

Do all these plants have flowers?

Do all plants have the same parts? What other parts can you label?

Things to do

Collect plant parts. Put them together. Make a big plant. Label the parts.

Dig deeper

Find out:
- what **petals**, thorns and bulbs are.

What's underground?

Plants need **roots**. Where are they? Draw a plant with roots.

Did you know?

- Some plants don't have leaves!

A cactus

Leaves and roots

Things to learn
- What plants use water and light for.
- What plants need to grow.

I wonder...

Are all flowers safe to eat?

Good enough to eat?

What do roots do?

Roots hold plants upright. They take in water from the soil.

Some plants store food in them. We eat them!

Can you name these roots?

Things to do

If you cut the root from a plant, do you think it will grow? If you cut the leaves off, what will happen? Try it and find out.

Dig deeper

Find out:
- what else we use plants for.

Did you know?
- The water lily has some of the biggest leaves in the world. You could sit on one like a boat.

What is a leaf for?

Plants need light. A leaf uses the light to help a plant grow. Without light a plant will die.

Thirsty plants

Your challenge

- To answer a question.
- To decide what to do.
- To follow instructions.
- To share what you found out.

A special place to walk and relax

Special places

A garden is a special place. It needs to be looked after. What makes it special? Why is water important?

What to do

Class 1 want to see how important water is. They give one plant water. They keep one plant dry. Can they give the plant too much water?

What you need

- a jug
- two **similar** plants

What to check

Now try it yourselves.

- Use two potted plants that are the same.
- Measure some water into a jug.
- Water one plant pot only.

What happens to each plant?

What did you find?

Imran's Plant

Ali's Plant

These are Class 1's plants. Which plant had the water? How can you tell?

Did you know?

- Some plants store water inside themselves.

Give me sunshine

Your challenge

- To ask a question.
- To share what you discover.
- To record what you see.

My grass is all yellow.

I don't think it's had enough light.

Oh. It's not had enough water then.

What to do

- Sheila and Habiba want to test who is right.
- They wet the grass.
- They cover one small area of grass with dark plastic.
- They leave the other area of grass in sunlight.

What you need

- two trays of plants
- a thick cloth
- some water

What do you think?

What to check

Try it yourselves.

- Water both trays of plants.
- Cover one tray with the cloth.
- Look at the plants every day.

What happens to the plants in each tray?

Sheila and Habiba drew these pictures:

	Day 1	Day 2	Day 3	Day 4	Day 5
Plants under cloth					
Plants in sunlight					

Which plants grew better?

How can you tell?

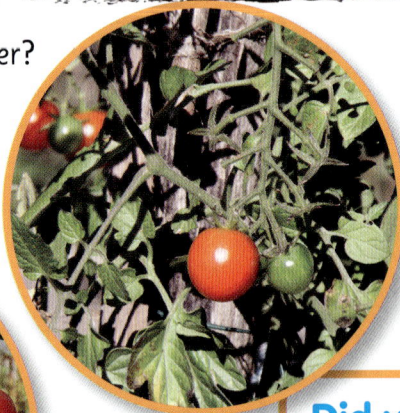

Which plant was grown in the warmer place?

Did you know?

- Plants grow best in warm places.

Seeds inside

Things to learn

- Where plants grow from.
- To explore how plants grow.
- To record your work.

I wonder...

What makes a seed start to grow?

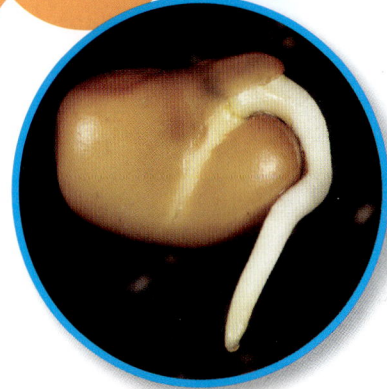

Is my plant alive?

We know plants are alive. Sometimes plants look dead but they contain seeds, which can grow into new plants.

Soy bean plant seed pods

Poppy seed pods

Which comes first?

When a seed is planted and watered, it grows. It sends out a root and then a **shoot**.

Things to do

Plant a seed. Watch how it grows. Draw pictures of it. Mix them up. Ask your friend to put them back in order.

Dig deeper

Find out:
- where the seeds are on a strawberry.

Did you know?

- Seeds can start to grow in the dark.

What have you learned?

- Where we find plants.
- The names of the parts of a plant.
- What some of the parts are for.
- How plants grow.
- How a seed starts to grow.

Find out more about…

- other animals' life cycles
- whether a plant is alive or not.

Check-up

How can you tell if a plant or animal is alive?

Even the weeds
in the garden are living plants.

The answer!

A weed is a plant that grows where we don't want it!

Unit 3: Sorting and using materials

What are materials? How do we use them? How do we choose the best materials?

What do you know?

- We have five **senses**.
- How to explore objects.
- The names of some **materials**.

Skills check

Can you...

- say what colour something is?
- group some objects together?
- describe common materials?

Words to learn

bendy	metal
cold	plastic
colour	properties
dry	rough
fabric	shape
hard	soft
heavy	waterproof
light	wet
material	wood

We use different materials to make different things

Let's find out...

Could you drink hot tea from a tea cup made of chocolate?

What's it like?

Things to learn

- What a material is.
- Using to explore materials.
- Use your senses.

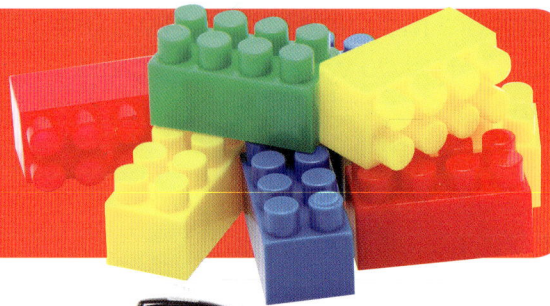

Which one?

You have five senses. Touch, taste, smell, hearing and sight. Which do you use to explore **materials**?

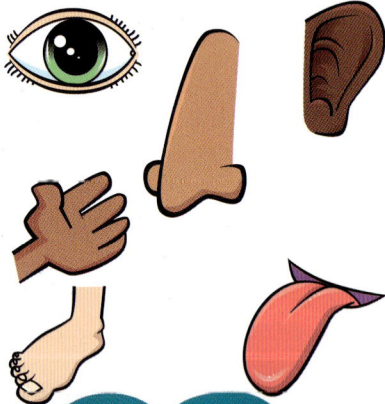

What words describe these objects?

Things to do

Close your eyes. Feel an object. Can you tell what it is? What is it made of? What clues were there?

I wonder...

What are the rarest materials?

Dig deeper

Find out:
- what materials are safe to taste.

Did you know?

- Material is not just **fabric** or cloth!

What words describe materials? 'Soft', 'shiny', and 'hard' are some.

A lot of materials

Things to learn

- To name some materials.
- To describe some materials.
- To explore materials and sort them into groups.

This spoon is made of a natural material – wood

Plastic is used to make lots of things

Natural or not?

Some materials are made by us. Some are found in nature. A wooden spoon is made from a natural material. A plastic spoon is not natural. What other natural materials can you name?

Dig deeper

Find out:
- what is made of plastic?

Things to do

Look at some materials. Sort them into two groups. What would you call them? Can you sort them any other way?

I wonder...

What is the most expensive material?

Did you know?

- Glass is made with sand.

Common materials

Your challenge

- To collect information.
- To record what you found out.
- To sort materials into groups.

Our school uniforms are made of materials.

Yes, and so is this desk.

But the desk isn't made of fabric like our uniforms.

But Materials aren't just fabrics!

What to do

Rohan and Anya decided to count all the materials they can. They find out which is the most common.

What you need

- a clipboard
- a pencil and some paper
- a digital camera

Object	Wood	Plastic	Paper	Fabric	Glass	Metal
🪑	✓					
Total						

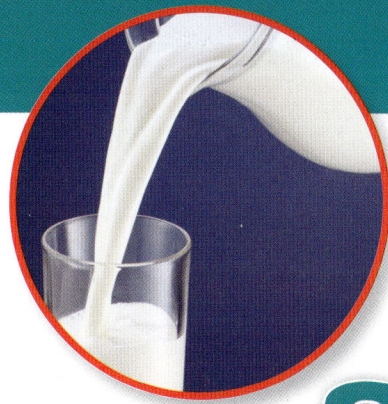

What to check

Now try it yourselves.

- Walk round the school. Look for different objects.
- Write down the name of each object.
- Decide what material it is made from.
- Count how many different materials you found.

Which material is the most common?

Things to do

Rohan and Anya drew this table of their results.

What material did Rohan and Anya find most of? Why do you think this is?

Object	Wood	Plastic	Paper	Fabric	Glass	Metal
🪑	✓					
📖			✓			
🪑		✓				
▭				✓		
🚪	✓					
🧰		✓				
▯					✓	
🧺		✓				
Total	2	3	1	1	1	0

The properties of materials

Things to learn

- Some properties of materials.
- To test the properties of a material.
- To share your ideas.

Magnets

Some materials are magnetic. A magnet will attract them.

Floating

Some materials **float** on water. Some materials sink

Things to do

- Test the **properties** of a range of materials.
- Test them with a magnet – does it attract them?
- Put them in water. Do they float or sink?
- Test them by dropping them. Do they bounce?
- Are they shiny? Can you see your face in them?
- What other tests can you do?

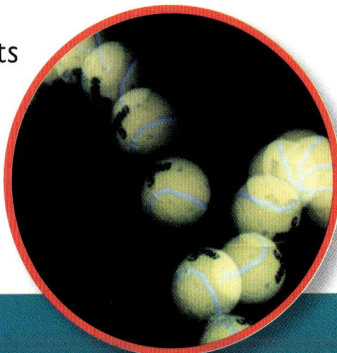

I wonder...

How **stretchy** is an elastic band?

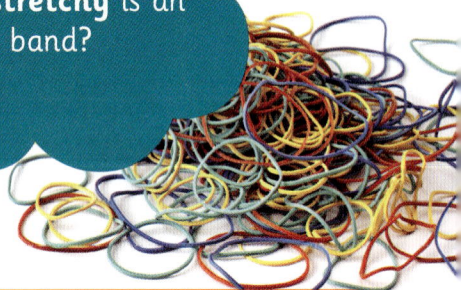

Dig deeper

Find out:
- how boats can be made from materials that sink.

Did you know?

- Not all metals are magnetic.

What's its job?

Things to learn

- Which materials are right for a job.
- To link materials to their properties.
- To explain what you know.

I wonder...

Would I like to wear **concrete** shoes?

Best for the job

Glass is used for windows. Light passes through it. Wood is strong. It is used for tables.

Things to do

Look at a house or a car. What materials are used? Why?

Which spoon?

Plastic bends in hot food. Metal gets hot. Wood burns. Which spoon is best?

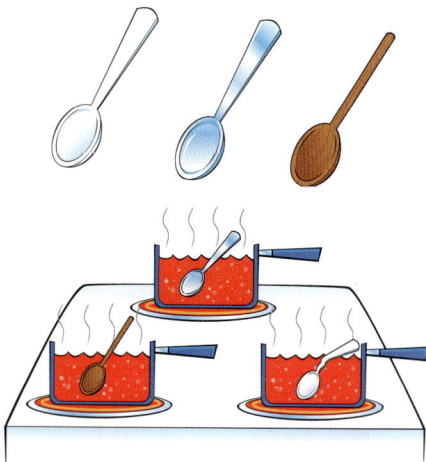

Which spoon should we use to stir the hot soup?

Dig deeper

Find out:
- what new materials scientists are inventing.

Did you know?

- The first cars had a wooden frame.

Don't get wet

I wonder…
Which materials are waterproof?

I'm soaked
Some materials stop water. They are **waterproof**.

Which clothes when?
Some clothes are better for some weathers. Which clothes would you wear in the rain? Why?

Paper isn't good at stopping water

Dig deeper
Find out:
- why an oilskin is called an oilskin.

Things to do
What does an umbrella do? Which material makes the best umbrella? What property must the material have?

Did you know?
- You can make cotton cloth waterproof with **wax**!

Paper

Things to learn

- What jobs a material can do.
- To sort paper into groups.
- To compare lots of different paper.

I wonder...

Who made the first paper? How?

Wooden books

Paper is made from wood. We can use old paper to make new paper.

We grow trees to make into paper

Different uses

Paper is very useful. It can do lots of jobs. How many jobs can you think of?

All of these are paper

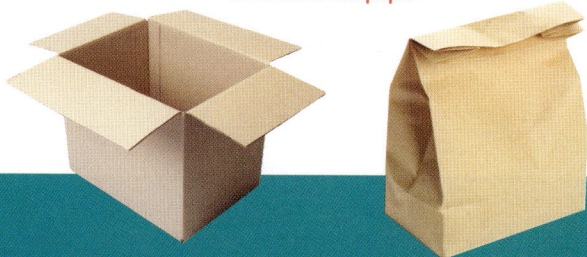

Things to do

Test different papers for their properties. Sort them into groups. Which is the best paper for wrapping?

Dig deeper

Find out:
- how many trees are needed to make one tonne of newspaper.

Did you know?

- You can eat rice paper!

All bagged up

Look at these bags. They are all useful. They all have different properties.

Benazir and Jamila have been shopping. They have to carry all these things home.

Which is the best bag to use?

What to do

Benazir and Jamila put the shopping into a bag. They want to see how much it holds. Are its handles strong enough?

What you need
- lots of bags
- some vegetables

What to check

Try it yourselves.

Decide what a shopping bag needs to be like. Should it be:
- waterproof?
- able to float?
- magnetic?
- strong?

How will you find the best one? What are its properties?

What did you find?

Benazir and Jamila found these results.

Some bags broke. Some bags tore.
The cloth bags was the strongest.

Did you know?

- It takes over two years for a plastic bag to rot.

Some rubbish is collected and buried

What have you learned?

- The names of some materials.
- How to recognize some materials by using your senses.
- The jobs that some materials can do.
- That one material can do many jobs.
- That one job can be done by many materials.
- Some properties of materials.

Check-up

Which group would you put this saucepan into?

If you touched these materials how would they feel?

Find out more about...

- Unusual materials like rubber.
- What happens to some materials in water.

The answer!

A cup made of chocolate wouldn't work for a hot drink. It would melt! It would also make the drink taste of chocolate!

Unit 4: Forces

What do you know?

- Words like 'strong' and 'weak', 'fast' and 'slow'.
- Words for directions like 'left' and 'right'.
- How to make something move.

Skills check

Can you...

- observe what happens?
- guess what will happen?

Forces make these things move

Let's find out...

Could you get dressed if you could only push, and not pull?

A pull is a force in action

Words to learn !

bend	push
change	slide
describe	slow down
forces	speed up
hop	stretch
jump	strong
observe	twist
pull	weak

Moving around

Things to learn

- Your left and right.
- How you can move.
- To follow instructions.

Simon says: 'Put your right arm up.'

Which is right?

Hold out both your hands. Put your thumbs out and your fingers in the air. One hand makes the letter 'L' for left. This is your left hand.

I wonder...

How else can my body move?

Things to do

Play 'Simon Says'. Did you follow the instructions correctly? What did you get wrong?

Dig deeper

Find out:
- which way is clockwise. Why is it called this?

Which way do the hands move?

Did you know?

- If you are left-handed, you can still be right-footed!

Moving things around

Things to learn
- How to make something move.
- The difference between a push and a pull.
- To answer a question.

I wonder...

Why is it easier to pull down than lift up?

Push me, pull me

Pushes and pulls are **forces**. A push moves something away from you. What does a pull do? Which **direction** does it move?

Dig deeper

Find out:
- what force keeps us on the ground.

Did you know?
- Some things can be both pushed and pulled.

Is he pushing or pulling the ball?

Things to do

Look around your classroom. Which things do you push to make them move? Which do you pull? Label them. Which do you push and pull?

Is a lift a push or a pull?

Using pushes and pulls

Your challenge
- To explore pushes and pulls in our lives.
- To collect **evidence** to answer a question.
- To share what you found out.

What to do

Gen and Sammi want to find out about pushes and pulls. Where are they used? They visit a playground. Then they visit a building site.

What you need
- a clipboard
- a camera

What to check

Now try it for yourselves.

- Visit a playground.
- Look where pushes and pulls are used.
- Draw some pictures.
- Mark all the pushes in blue.
- Mark all the pulls in red.
- Count them.
- Are there more pushes or more pulls?

What did you find?

Gen and Sammi found forces in the building site.

Builders use strong forces.

When do they push? When do they pull?

Why are buildings sites dangerous? Why must you KEEP OUT?

Did you know?

- Diggers are used to move soil. They push and pull.

How far can you go?

Your challenge
- To guess what will happen.
- To measure carefully.
- To share what you found.

Why does your car keep going further than mine?

What are you doing differently to me?

I don't know.

I am just pushing it like this.

What to do

Abdul and Safia test different ways of pushing their cars. They push some hard. They push some gently.

Whose car goes furthest? Why?

What you need
- some toy cars
- ruler or tape measure

What could Abdul do to catch up?

What to check

Now try it yourselves.

- Guess how far your car will travel with a small push.
- Push it.
- Measure how far it went.
- Were you right?
- Give it a bigger push.
- Then an even bigger push.

What happens?

What did you find?

Abdul and Safia found these results.

Push size	Distance car went
Small	15 footsteps
Medium	25 footsteps
Large	30 footsteps
Very large	50 footsteps

Which push made the car go furthest? What should Abdul do to make his car keep up with Safia's?

As well as footsteps they also measured how far the car went with a ruler.

Did you know?
- The dung beetle can push over a thousand times its own weight!

Slow down

Things to learn

- How to make something speed up.
- How to stop something.
- To explain what happens.

I wonder…
How fast does a jet plane travel?

Ouch!

This skateboarder was travelling very fast. He fell off. He has hurt himself.

Things to do

What happens if you go too fast? Set up a ramp, car and a block. Let the car go. What happens to the block if you push the car?

Dig deeper

Find out:
- what is the fastest animal on Earth.

Did you know?

- The faster a car goes, the longer it takes to stop.

Other ways of moving things

Things to learn

- How to move objects without touching them.
- How wind and water make things move.
- To test ideas

I wonder...

How can moving water generate electricity?

Is the wind invisible?

You can't see the wind. But it makes things move. We use the wind to generate electricity or **grind** corn.

Things to do

Make a paper windmill. Blow it. Blow harder. What happens? What does the air do?

Dig deeper

Find out:
- how wind generates electricity.

Water wheels

Water makes things move. It pushes the water wheel round.

Did you know?

- Wind in a **hurricane** can lift up houses.

Which way next?

Things to learn
- How to make something move.
- How forces change direction.

No need to change direction here!

Forces

Forces make things move. Forces make things slow down and stop. Forces make things change direction.

How do you change direction in these sports?

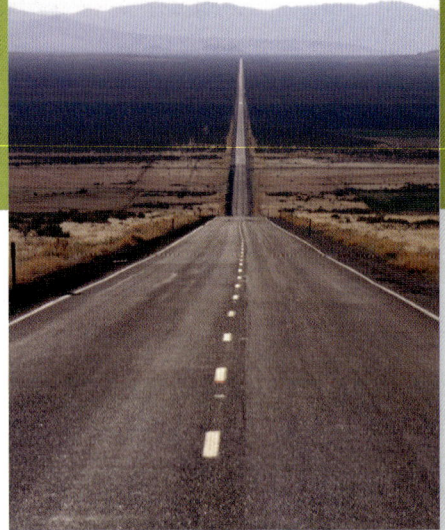

Things to do

Roll a ball. Make it change direction. What do you have to do? How can you make the ball stop? What forces do you use?

Dig deeper
Find out:
- how a bicycle changes direction.

Did you know?
- Changing direction needs a push or a pull.

I wonder...
How does an aeroplane change direction?

Blow football

Things to learn

- How to change the direction of something.
- To problem solve.
- To say what you have learnt.

What is going on in this picture?

Things to do

Make a football game. What forces do you use to play?

Tell a friend about it. Use words about forces.

Dig deeper

Find out:
- what forces you need to swim.

I wonder...

What forces do you need to move around school?

Did you know?

- Footballers use many different forces.

What have you learned?

- About pushes and pulls.
- How to move things without touching them.
- How to slow things down.
- How to make something go faster or further.
- How to make something change direction.

Jet planes such as this hold world speed records

Find out more about...

- speed and safety
- world speed records.

Check-up

A marble run uses forces.

What's the longest marble run you can make?

The answer!

If you could only use pushes and no pulls, you wouldn't be able to get dressed in the morning. Try it!

Unit 5: Sound

There are many ways of making sounds. Some sounds are quiet. Some sounds are loud. Some loud sounds can harm your ears.

What do you know?

- The sense we use for hearing.
- To recognize the names of some sounds.

Words to learn

direction	loud
echo	low
faint	music
high	sense
instruments	soft
listen	source

Let's find out...

What if we lived on a planet without words? How else could we use sounds?

Sounds all around

Things to learn

- How we hear.
- How to describe sounds.
- To recognize our voices.

I wonder...

What would it be like if you couldn't hear? What would you miss?

Our senses

We have five senses. We use our ears for hearing.

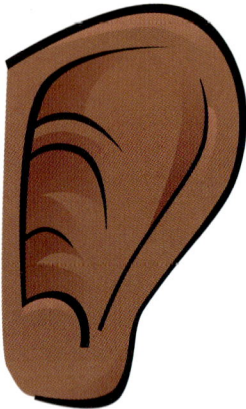

Things to do

Stand in a circle. **Blindfold** one person. Put them in the middle of the circle. Someone in the circle makes a noise. Can they point at the noise?

Dig deeper

Find out:
- how a loud noise can damage your ears.

Who is it?

Can you tell who calls you? Can you tell if they are happy? How? This person is the source of the sound.

Did you know?

- You can feel some sounds.

Can you hear if you cover your ears?

I can feel it bumping up and down!

Your challenge
- To make a prediction.
- To collect information.
- To record what you found out.

Oh my poor head. I have such a headache.

I don't think it is. I'll try the yard.

My classroom is quieter.

But all the children are playing there.

What to do

The teacher walks round the school. She **listens** carefully. She counts the sounds she hears in each place. She chooses a quiet place to sit in.

What is the quietest place in school?

What you need
- a clipboard
- a pencil and paper

Place name	Number of sounds

What to check

Try it for yourselves.

- Walk round the school.
- Listen for different sounds.
- Write them down.
- Count them.

How many sounds did you hear?

Which was the quietest place?

What did you find?

The teacher found these results.

Place name	Number of sounds
yard	children, birds, wind, cars = 4
canteen	washing up, workers, fridges = 3
teacher's lounge	teachers, coffee machine = 2

Which place did the teacher find quietest?

Where can you sit quietly?

Where can you make a lot of noise?

Did you know?

- The Blue Whale makes the loudest sound of any animal!

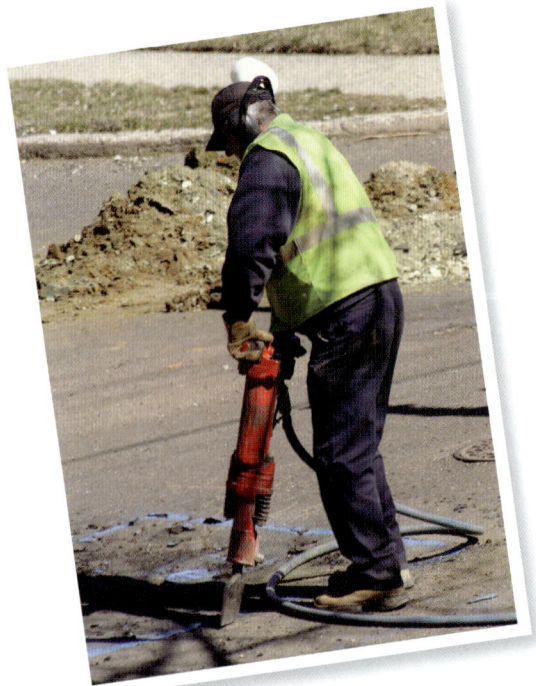

Protect your ears from loud sounds

Music makers

I wonder...
How can people with poor hearing be helped?

Crash, bang, wallop

All these instruments make sounds. But what are they called? What sort of sounds do they make?

How can you make sounds from these?

Things to do

You have to do something to an instrument to make a sound. You have to play it.

Put the instruments into groups by how you play them. Are there any in two groups?

scrape   blow   pluck   hit with sticks or hands

Dig deeper
Find out:
- what instrument makes the loudest noise.

Make your own

You can make your own instruments. Use straws, elastics bands and boxes. What musical instrument can you make?

Did you know?
- Some sounds, like fingernails down a board, can make you shiver.

All ears

Things to learn
- How we can hear better.
- Why we need to listen carefully.

I wonder...
Can sound travel round corners?

Danger danger

How do you know a police car is coming? What does it sound like as it goes by?

Dig deeper
Find out:
- why we should stop look and listen before we cross the road.

Did you know?
- You can hear better through the ground than the air!

Animal ears

Animals have ears like us. They have different sized ears. Some have big ears to listen for danger.

Things to do

Do you need both ears? Cover one ear. Listen to your friends. Where are they? Listen with both ears. Why is this better?

I can hear three horses, one with a loose shoe.

Is bigger better?

Your challenge
- To suggest ideas to test.
- To make a prediction.
- To see if you were right or not.

What to do

Ali and his friends want to see if bigger ears hear better. They roll up paper and put it to their ears. They listen. They then make bigger cones with paper. They listen.

I can hear something.

I can't hear anything.

That's because you've got small ears.

What you need
- different sized cones
- a drum or tape player

Which piece of paper should we use?

What to check

Try it yourselves.

- Take three different sized pieces of paper.
- Roll into a cone and tape them.
- Put the small end over your ear.
- Listen carefully.

Which size of cone makes the sounds loudest?

What did you find?

Ali found that big ears made the sounds the loudest.

They want to make an even better ear. They want to hear sounds far away. What should they do?

Did you know?

- Some people can wiggle their ears. Can you?

Sounds far away

Things to learn

- There are many sources of sound.
- How sound changes with distance.
- To share what was found out.

I wonder...

How far can sound travel?

How loud?

The bell is very loud. But some children in the yard can't hear it.

The bell is the source of the sound.

We hear loud, high sounds from far away.

Things to do

Stand in a line away from the sound. Raise your hand when you hear the sound. What happens as you get further from the sound?

Dig deeper

Find out:
- if sounds travel under water.

Did you know?

- An elephant's 'rumble' can be heard 10 km away.

Diminishing distances

Your challenge

- To collect information.
- To answer questions.
- To share your ideas.

What to do

How far does sound travel?
Sarah and Pritpal play a radio
in the yard. They see how far
away they can hear it.

I think I can hear the best.

I can hear from a long **distance**.

No you can't, I can!

But so can I!

What you need

- a radio or MP3 player
- a large space

What to check

Try it yourselves.

- Stand across the yard.
- Listen for the sound.
- Move away from the sound. Stop when you can't hear it.
- Measure how far you are from the sound **source**.

What has Pritpal found out?

What did you find?

Sound travels. The further you are from the sound, the quieter it is.

When you are far from the sound, you cannot hear it.

As you come closer, you can hear it again.

Imagine you are climbing a high tower, like the tower below. Would the sound of the traffic in the street fade as you climbed?

Why?

Did you know?

- Sound can travel 20 km in one minute!

What have you learned?

- Sound comes from a source.
- We hear with our ears.
- Sounds get quieter the further we are away.
- Loud noises can damage our ears.
- Big ears help animals hear dangers.
- Sound travels out from its source in all directions.

Loud sounds can damage your ears

Find out more about…

- How a megaphone works.
- How sound travels.

Check-up

Make a string telephone. Pull the string tight. Speak softly into the cup.

These children can hear each other

The answer!

You might make different sounds. Many animals make sounds. The sounds are signals.

Unit 1: Ourselves and other animals checklist

What do you know?
- Think about these statements
- Which do you know? Which can you do?

- I know if something is alive or not
- I can say how things are different or the same
- I can name parts of my body
- I know what we need to grow healthy
- I can say what my five senses are
- I can describe how we all change as we grow
- I can look carefully at things (observe)

Unit 2: Growing plants checklist

What do you know?

- Think about these statements
- Which do you know? Which can you do?

- I know where to look for plants
- I can name the parts of a plant
- I know what some of the parts of a plant are for
- I can make a seed grow
- I can describe how plants grow
- I can list some plants we eat
- I can look carefully at things
- I can try to show others what I found out

What do you know?

- Think about these statements
- Which do you know? Which can you do?

- I can name some materials
- I can list some of the jobs that some materials can do
- I know that one material can do many jobs
- I also know that one job can be done by many materials
- I can describe some properties of materials
- I can sort materials into groups
- I can name the groups I used
- I can test materials to find out which is best for the job
- I can describe what I found out

Unit 4: Forces checklist

What do you know?
- Think about these statements
- Which do you know? Which can you do?

- I recognize how useful pushes and pulls are
- I recognize if something is a push or a pull
- I know how to move things without touching them
- I can make something change direction
- I know how to make something go faster or further
- I know how to slow something down
- I can make a guess of what will happen
- I can follow instructions
- I know my left and right
- I can say what I found out from a test
- I am starting to measure
- I know it is sometimes dangerous to stop something moving

Unit 5: Sound checklist

What do you know?
- Think about these statements
- Which do you know? Which can you do?

- I know that there are many sources of sound
- I know which sense we use to hear with
- I can describe different sounds
- I recognize different sounds
- I can describe what happens to sound as we get further away from it
- I know that loud noises can damage our ears
- I know that we hear better with bigger ears
- I can describe why two ears are better than one
- I know how to make lots of different sounds
- I can describe what I found out
- I can share what I found out
- I can guess what I think will happen

Glossary

adult a grown-up

alive able to grow, move and respond to surroundings

attract pull towards

blind unable to see

blindfold cover someones eyes with, for example, a cloth

concrete hard material used for building

deaf unable to hear

different not the same

direction the way to go, e.g. left, right, backwards, forwards

distance the space between two things

evidence things you hear, see or discover

fabric material/cloth for making clothes

float does not sink.

flower the part of a plant that produces seeds

forces to make objects move, e.g. push or pull

fruit part of a plant that contains the seeds

grind break into small pieces

hear/listen we use our ears for this

human the type of animal we are

hurricane very strong wind

leaf part of a plant that produces its food

material what everything is made of, e.g. plastic, wood, metal, glass

petals brightly coloured part of a flower

properties quality of materials

root the underground part of a plant

seed grows into a new plant.

senses parts of the body (ear, eye, skin, tongue, nose) that tell you what is going on

shoot new green part of a plant

sight we use our eyes for this

similar almost the same

smell we use our nose for this

source where sound or light come from

stem the part of plant that holds up the leaves and the flower

stretchy getting bigger when pulled

taste we use our mouths and tongue for this

touch we use our hands and skin for this

tree a woody plant

waterproof keeps water out

wax used for candles

weed plant growing where it is not wanted

Index